Infinite Moral Compass

Antoninus Michaelus Angelus

Antoninus Michaelus Angelus

Infinite Moral Compass

∞

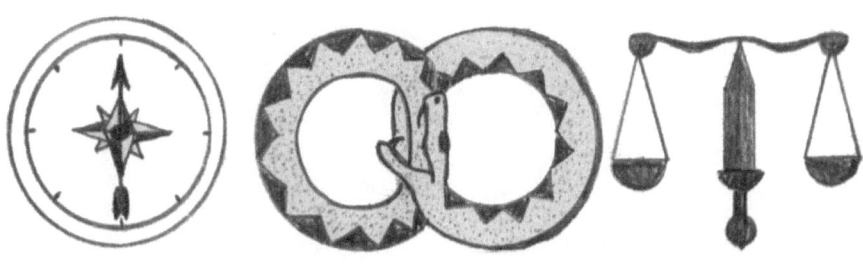

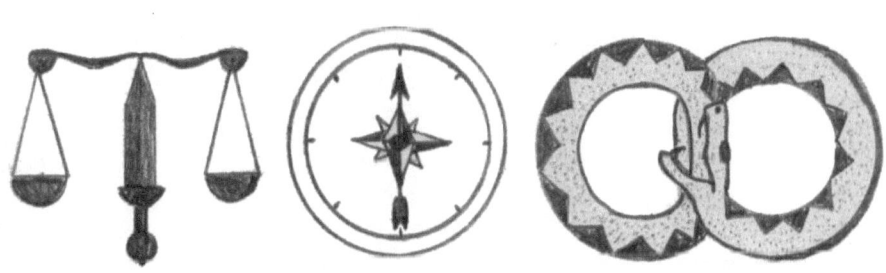

The Environment

The Liberating Arts of Life & Death start with The Environment, by way of
Sensory Input & Athletics.

The Environment Attaches & Detaches;
When It attaches, Electricity is transferred.

Electricity determines Frequency;
Frequency determines Vibration;
Vibration determines Movement;
Movement determines Energy;
Energy determines Current;
Current determines Power;
Power determines Detachment;
Detachment determines One.

In The Infinite Landscape of Nature, there are no contradictions;
Only Paradoxes of Life & Death.

The Trivium

From The Environment, The Liberating Arts of Life & Death transform into The Trivium, by way of Thoughts & Philosophies.

Grammar, by way of Symbols;
Symbols, by way of Visions.

Logic, by way of Structure;
Structure, by way of Reason.

Rhetoric, by way of Persuasion;
Persuasion, by way of Communication.

Reading Arts;
Thinking Arts;
Linguistic Arts;
Liberation Arts.

The Quadrivium

From The Trivium, The Liberating Arts of Life & Death transform into The Quadrivium, by way of Expressions & Artistry.

Arithmetic, by way of Numbers;
Numbers, by way of Calculations.

Geometry, by way of Shapes;
Shapes, by way of Formations.

Music, by way of Numbers in Motions;
Numbers in Motions, by way of Vibrations.

Astronomy, by way of Shapes in Motions;
Shapes in Motions, by way of All.

Crafting Arts;
Exploring Arts;
Naturalizing Arts;
Expressing Arts;
Liberating Arts.

Building Foundations

Infinite

What is Infinite? Endlessly Microcosmic & Endlessly Macrocosmic.
How is Infinite? Endlessly Wondered.
Why is Infinite? Endless Wonder.
When is Infinite? Now, by way of Endlessly Wondering.
Where is Infinite? Endlessly Everywhere.

Moral

What is a Moral? One's Evolved Principle of Good & Not-Good.
How is a Moral? One's way of Conscience & Consciousness & Sub-
Consciousness.
Why is a Moral? One's 5 Senses & Trivium & Quadrivium & Creations.
Where is a Moral? One's Sub-Consciousness & Consciousness & Conscience.
When is a Moral? Now, by way of Infinite Beginnings & Endings.

Compass

What is a Compass? That which aligns to Magnetic North or South of an
Electromagnetic Field.
How is a Compass? One's Magnetic Conduction inside All Electromagnetic
Fields.
Why is a Compass? For One to Balance in All.
Where is a Compass? In All of Alls, by way of Infinite Ones.
When is a Compass? Now, by way of Infinite Dimensional Electromagnetism.

Creating Morals

Morals, by way of Needs;
Needs, by way of Values;
Values, by way of Beliefs;
Beliefs, by way of Habits;
Habits, by way of Free Will;
Free Will, by way of Attention;
Attention, by way of Sensory Input;
Sensory Input, by way of Environment;
Environment, by way of Electromagnetism;
Electromagnetism, by way of All;
All, by way of One.

Adjusting The Labyrinth;
Adjusting The Direction;
Adjusting The Way;
Adjusting The Maze;
Adjusting The Path;
Adjusting The Compass.

The Evolving One Among All

Survival, by way of the 5 Senses, Athletically;
The 5 Senses filter into The One Athlete.

Fame, by way of The Trivium, Philosophically;
Grammar & Logic & Rhetoric filter into The One Philosopher.

Fortune, by way of The Quadrivium, Artistically;
Arithmetic & Geometry & Music & Astronomy filter into The One Artist.

Purpose, by way of Creation, Creatively;
Evolving Reasons To Create Morals filter into The One Creator.

Morals & Humans

Every One wants to know what another One's Morals are, yet:
Many do not like Thinking;
Many do not like Expressing;
Many do not like Creating.

What Good & Not-Good is, Conscience knows.
How Good & Not-Good is, Conscience & Consciousness knows.
Why Good & Not-Good is, Conscience & Consciousness knows.
When Good & Not-Good is, Conscience & Sub-Consciousness knows.
Where Good & Not-Good is, Conscience & Sub-Consciousness & Consciousness knows.
Who Good & Not-Good is, One & All.

For where there is Good, there is an equal Not-Good to level All.

Determining Beginnings & Endings

Morals determine Beliefs & Values;
Beliefs & Values determine Decisions;
Decisions determine Motivations;
Motivations determine Interests;
Interests determine Self-Worth;
Self-Worth determines Self-Awareness;
Self-Awareness determines Moral Feedback;
Moral Feedback determines Feedback-Attention to Morals;
Feedback-Attention to Morals determine Beliefs & Values;
Beliefs & Values determines Thoughts;
Thought determines Motion;
Motion determines Emotion;
Emotion determines Devotion;
Devotion determines Creation;
Creation determines Everything;
Everything determines Dissolution;
Dissolution determines Endings & Beginnings.

A Dawn of One

To see is to discover One;
To see One is to discover Symbol;
To see Symbols is to discover Pattern;
To see Patterns is to discover Arithmetic;
To see Arithmetics is to discover Language;
To see Languages is to discover Logic;
To see Logics is to discover Communication;
To see Communications is to discover Expression;
To see Expressions is to discover Creation;
To see Creations is to discover All;
To see All is to discover One.

Connecting dots that cannot be unconnected;
Learning something that cannot be unlearned;
Decisions in Time, consequently changing Time itself.

Wisdom

Showing experience, knowledge, and Good judgment;
A state of Being.

On a Planet where many are excessively consuming Sensory Information, few are
Foraging-For or Filling One's Self with Wisdom.

Productivity, by way of Success;
Success, by way of Good Judgment;
Good Judgment, by way of Wisdom;
Wisdom, by way of Failure;
Failure, by way of Not-Good Judgement;
Not-Good Judgement, by way of Consumption-Only.

Net Good Morals | 5-3-4-∞

All Belief Systems can have both Good & Not-Good Morals;
One Belief System can have Theoretical & Practical Net Good Morals versus another.

Athletics is a Universal Body Belief System, by way expressing of the Five Senses.

Philosophy is a Universal Mind Belief System, by way of expressing Grammar, Logic, and Rhetoric.

Artistry is a Universal Nature Belief System, by way of expressing Arithmetic, Geometry, Music, and Astronomy.

Creatorship is a Universal Belief System, by way of expressing Inventions, Innovations, and Ingenuity, Ad Infinitum.

Universal Morals exist, by way of Producing, Planning, Prioritizing, Practicing, and Performing Net Good outcomes.

Is this One, Planet, Solar System, Galaxy, or Universe contributing to All Universes' Net Good Morals?

Questions

Questioning is as important as knowing;
Knowing to question is as important as believing what One knows;
Questioning what One knows is as important as knowing what One believes.

All One's Beliefs are pliable; and One's Belief is always among All Beliefs.

Why?
How?
What?
Where?
Who?
When?

Now.

Autodidact

Learn how to learn.
Learn how to learn constantly.
Learn how to question.
Learn how to question One's 5 Senses.
Learn how to question One's Thoughts.
Learn how to question One's Emotions.
Learn how to question One's Beliefs.
Learn how to question One's Values.
Learn how to question One's Beginnings.
Learn how to question One's Endings.
Learn how to question One's Everything One has ever known.

This is living truly;
Living truly is living Now;
Now is the Truth;
Now is the Creation of Truth;
The Creation of Truth is Living;
Truly Living is The Truth.

Misguidance can be performed, truthfully;
Mistakes can be made, truthfully;
All want to be able to See, Hear, Feel, Smell, Taste, Think, Know, Feel, and Create
The Truth.

To not be Intentionally Creating, this is to be Misguided to Not-Good.
To be Intentionally Destroying, this is to be Willfully Not-Good.

Educate

Educare is to bring up; to rise; to nourish.
Educere is to lead out; to draw out; to bring from.
Educatum is the act of teaching; training.
Educatus is to bring up; rear.
Educatio is the breeding; a bringing up; a rearing.
Educate is to train Sub-Consciousness & Consciousness & Conscience.

Self-Education, by way of One;
One is in All;
To Educate One is to Educate All;
All Educates The One;
Education is The One's All, by way of One's Self-Education;
All must be Educated by every One.

Infinite Origins

Discovering the Primary Citation is nearly impossible;
All sources come from previous sources;
One can only come to Reason with what is Probable.

Who told One what to believe?
Has One ever heard another One say that?
If One tells One what to believe, then who told that One?

All Morals are perpetually adjusting to its Moment Of Time, Now.

Communication Of One

All is Communication;
All is Language;
All is Body, Speech, Writing;
All is Sensory Input.

All Sensory Input becomes Symbol;
Symbol becomes Grammar;
Grammar becomes Logic;
Logic becomes Rhetoric;
This is the Trivium of The Liberating Arts of Life & Death.

Arithmetic becomes Geometry;
Geometry becomes Music;
Music becomes Astronomy;
Astronomy is All;
All is Expression of One;
This is the Quadrivium of The Liberating Arts of Life & Death.

If One can, Create;
One can Create All;
Because The All has already Created The One.

War

Left Hemisphere vs. Right Hemisphere;
Intelligence Quotient vs. Emotional Quotient;
Thought vs. Emotion;
Logic vs. Reason.

The War is inside of every One, between balancing the Right & Left & Bottom & Top.

One Creates their own War into The Environment;
The Environment creates Local Battles;
Local Battles Create larger scale Planetary Warfare.

All Wars are Wars of Environments;
All Wars are Wars of Thoughts;
All Wars are Wars of Emotions;
All Wars are Wars of Creations;
All Wars are Wars of Brains;
All Wars are Wars of Beliefs;
All Wars are Wars of Values;
All Wars are Wars of Morals;
All Wars are Wars of Wars.

∞

∞

Amygdala

One's Sensory Input causes Motivations & Emotions.
One's Sensory Input can cause Fear & Anxiety & Aggression & Depression.

Regarding The Animal Brain:
Environment comes To One; One reacts To All.

Regarding Point Of View:
Electromagnetism comes to One; One reacts to All.

Regarding Regards:
Sub-Consciousness & Consciousness & Conscience are One.
The Environment & Mind & Body is One among The Infinite Ones & Alls.

Without This, nothing after follows:
Autonomic Responses;
Hormonal Secretions;
Arousal;
Emotional Response;
Memory.

It decides before One's Consciousness knows.

Environmental Feedback Loops

Environments are Data Input;
Thoughts are Electromagnetic Fields;
Emotions are Biochemical Messengers;
Creations are New Data for the Environment.

All Systems perpetually use Data Feedback Loops to Create New Morals;
New Morals are New Data for the Environment;
Environments are Feedback Loops;
All is Feedback Looping.

Nature's Cycles create maps for One to navigate throughout;
All flows in The Cosmic Ocean;
One is trolling along on The Infinite Maritime of All.

Addiction

Environment creates Dopamine;
Dopamine creates Attention;
Attention creates Energy;
Energy creates Life;
Life creates Death.

The Addiction to Living;
The Addiction to Dying;
How deceivingly the same they are!

Sight & Ocular & Eye

Sight is the transfer of Ocular Sensory Input from the Eye;
This is One Seeing.

The Occipital Lobe creates The Vision;
This is One Seeing.

When Need & Want is not Now;
This is Observing.

Sound & Auditory & Ear

Vibration is the transfer of Auditory Sensory Input from the Ear;
This is One Hearing.

The Cochlea creates The Sound;
This is One Hearing.

When Need & Want is not Now;
This is Listening.

Touch & Tactile & Skin

Tactile Signals are the transfer of Electricity through Neurons;
This is One Touching.

The Somatosensory Cortex creates Electromagnetic Fields;
This is One Touching.

When Need & Want is not Now;
This is Feeling.

Scent & Olfactory & Nose

Scent is the transfer of Olfactory Sensory Input from the Nose;
This is One Smelling.

The Olfactory Bulb creates An Environment;
This is One Smelling.

When Need & Want is not Now;
This is Breathing.

Taste & Gustatory & Tongue

Life is the transfer of Gustatory Sensory Input from the Tongue;
This is One Tasting.

The Death transforms Life;
This is One Tasting.

When Need & Want is not Now;
This is Ingesting.

Genes & Epigenomes

Gene
Nucleotides;
Adenine & Thymine;
Cytosine & Guanine.

One's Code;
The Code of Potential;
The Potential of Chance;
The Chance of Change;
The Change of One;
The One in All.

Epigenome
The Environmentally Innovated;
The Environmentally Willed;
The Environmentally Wanted;
The Environmentally Focused;
The Environmentally Needed;
The Server or Slaver.

One's Environments determine Genes;
One's Genes determine Potentials;
One's Potentials determine Variations;
One's Variations determine Epigenomes;
One's Epigenomes determine Now;
Now determines The Future, Ad Infinitum.

∞

Memes

One creates, then serves;
One receives, then shares;
One receives, then recreates;
Ad Infinitum.

Environmental Information trains All;
All trains One;
The cycles Repeat & Change;
Ad Infinitum.

Systems, by way of Operational Information;
Operational Information, by way of Informational Input;
Informational Input, by way of The Quadrivium;
The Quadrivium, by way of The Trivium;
The Trivium, by way of The Environment;
Ad Infinitum.

Brainwaves

Sleeping in Delta;
Awakening in Alpha;
Thinking in Beta;
Navigating in Theta;
Creating in Gamma;
The Frequencies of Life & Death, Now.

Stages of Times;
Cycles of Lives;
Resonances of Frequencies;
Liquid of Oscillating Frequency Fields;
Inside of The Ocean of The Invisible;
Geomagnetics & Electromagnetics;
Geoelectric Pulsations;
Between Planet & Ionosphere.

Technological Advance increases;
Electromagnetic Pollution increases;
How One is & All become, Electromagnetically Harmonized & Dissonant.

Cybernetics

The Art of Steering.

Sensory Input, by way of Environmental Feedback;
Thought, by way of Sensory Input;
Motion, by way of Thought;
Emotion, by way of Motion;
Devotion, by way of Emotion;
Creation, by way of Devotion;
Environmental Feedback, by way of Creation.

One's Now in Time can be traversed.
Chart, Navigate, Steer, Repeat.
Sense, Compare, Adjust, Repeat.

∞

Biomechatronics

The Art of Bionic Living.

Osseointegration, by way of Bone & Planet.
Array of Microtubes, by way of Imitation.
Electrode Interconnections, by way of Desires.
Electronic Modules, by way of Imagination.
Biofeedback, by way of Electromyographic Signals.
Muscling, by way of Mind.
Neuron Development, by way of Necessity.
Optogenetics, by way of Sensory Enhancement.

One can create The Cyborg.
Discover, Innovate, Solve, Repeat.
Think, Embody, Experience, Repeat.

Augments

The Art of Biosynthetic Tooling.

Metabolic Preservation, by way of Exoskeletons.
Ocular Enhancements, by way of Crafted Lenses.
Restorative Ambulation, by way of Functionalities.

One's Senses were Thought to have Emotional limits.
Discover, Decide, Do, Repeat.
Theorize, Test, Become, Repeat.

Liquid Universe

Water substrates;
Copper substrates;
Silicon substrates;
Gallium Arsenide substrates.

Packets of Positive & Negative Electromagnetic Energy;
Fractally Larger & Smaller;
Envisioned in One & All.

To imagine All as a drop of water;
To imagine all as Electromagnetic Energy Waves;
To imagine All as a substrate.

All is Movement;
Movement is The Medium;
The Medium is Liquid;
Liquid is Matter;
Matter is Energy;
Energy is Substrate.

∞

Time & Space Dimensions

The 1st Dimension is Length;
The 2nd Dimension is Width;
The 3rd Dimension is Depth;
The 4th Dimension is Space;
The 5th Dimension is All.

Fractally Infinite in smaller Dimensions are the eyes of the Microcosm;
Fractally Infinite in larger Dimensions are the eyes of the Macrocosm.

All Time is relative to those observing any Dimension;
All observation is relative to those in any Dimension.

The Planet is flying through the 4th Dimension;
Time flies Within & Away when One is Living & Dying.

Art

Ars & Artem;
The Arm of Human;
The Skills of Crafting & Creating.

Artifact & Artificial;
Crafted & Created by The Arm of Human;
The Creations by The Artist.

Artificial Intelligence is only as Moral as The Artist's Creatorship.

Communication

Language, by way of The Body;
Language, by way of The Calligraphy;
Language, by way of The Oratory.

All Language in One, misleading is inevitable;
One Language in All, misunderstanding is inevitable.

Parts of Speech, by way of The Language;
Noun, Pronoun, Adjective, Verb, Adverb, Adposition, Conjunction, Interjection,
Numeral, Article, Determiner, Compound, Demonstrative, Intensifier, Interrogative,
Portmanteau, Orthography, Syntax, Ad Infinitum.

Abecedary is Number;
Number is Nature;
Nature is Law;
Law is All;
All is Public;
Public is Philosophic;
Philosophic is Rhetoric;
Rhetoric is Syntax;
Syntax is Language.

If Communication is impossible, then Dissolution is inevitable.

Cognitive Dissonance

When One observes incongruent Sensory Inputs, Thoughts, Beliefs, Values, Morals, One, or All.

Cognitive
The processes of Understandings & Overstandings, by way of Environmental Sensory Inputs, Thoughts, Motions, Emotions, Devotions, and Creations.

Dissonance
Devoid of Harmony between One's Understandings & Overstandings in The All.

As relating to Ideas & Focuses & Decisions & Motions & Emotions & Devotions & Creations, One's Sensory Inputs, Thoughts, Beliefs, Values, Morals, or All determine Congruency & Incongruency.

If One is Attentive, Energetic, and Lively in All, then Cognitive Dissonance is inevitable.

Life & Death being the same is Cognitive Dissonance.

Beliefs

The Environment can change Beliefs;
Can perceive information as True;
Can create Truths that can be Harmonious.

Free Will can change Beliefs;
Can analyze Beliefs;
Can question Beliefs;
Can decide Beliefs;
Can create Habitual Beliefs.

One is constantly Quantifying Beliefs;
There's never a single Belief Quantity.

How can Beliefs be measured?
Good & Not-Good Outcomes.

Attention to Ideas;
Attention to Visions;
Attention to Beliefs;
Attention to Values;
Attention to Morals.

Attention is Health;
Attention is Wealth.

Values

Beliefs can change Values;
Can Focus on a Value;
Can Decide a Value as Useful;
Can Reason a Value as Worthy.

Free Will can change Values;
Can analyze Values;
Can question Values;
Can decide Values;
Can create Habitual Values.

One is constantly Evaluating;
Constantly, One is Re-Evaluating.

How can Values be measured?
Good & Not-Good Outcomes.

Beliefs transform into Values;
Values transform into Energy, by way of Re-Evaluating;
Values transform Energy into Focuses;
Values transform Energy into Decisions;
Values transform Energy into Reasons.

What's the Usefulness & Worthiness to One?
What's the Usefulness & Worthiness to All?

Needs

Certainty is for the Honorable;
This is Thoughtfully Good.

Uncertainty is for the Courageous;
This is Powerfully Good.

Connection is for the Committed;
This is Inspirationally Good.

Growth is for the Autodidactic;
This is Liberatingly Good.

Contribution is for the Server;
This is Devotionally Good.

Significance is for The One;
This is Selfishly Good.

Creation is for The All;
This is Mysteriously Good.

Just

Just Because
Justice's Effect, by way of Cause.

Ius: A Right, Legal Right, Law.
Iustus: Upright, Righteous, Equitable; in accordance with Law, Lawful; True, Proper; Perfect, Complete.
Just: Morally Upright, Righteous in the eyes of The Universe; Equitable, Impartial, Fair.

One is Cause;
Cause is Probability;
Probability is All;
All is Nature;
Nature is Balance;
Balance is Justice;
Justice is Effect;
Effect is Change;
Change is Inevitable.

Positive & Negative;
Hot & Cold;
In & Out;
Up & Down;
Balanced & Not-Balanced;
Just & Not-Just;
Good & Not-Good.

Laws are still executed by One & All, Now.

∞

ism

Collectivism
The practice or principle of giving priority to All over each One in The All.
Giving priority to The All over One causes large quantities of Good & Not-Good
Outcomes, by way of the Value of The All.

Individualism
The practice or principle of giving priority of One over The All.
Giving priority to One over The All causes large quantities of Good & Not-Good
Outcomes, by way of the Value of The One.

Infinitism
The practice or principle of giving priority to the Infinitely-Evolving Morality of
One over The All.
Giving priority to The Infinitely-Evolving Morality of One & All to serve The All,
by way of The All to become as The Infinitely-Evolving One is.

One starts All;
All start new Ones;
All does not need One, yet One needs All;
One does not need All, yet All needs One.

All can Harmonize in The Liberating Arts of Life & Death;
If not, then Dissonance is inevitable.

Intention

To desire & to be pleased to cause Suffering is Not-Good.
To desire & to be pleased to cause Death is Not-Good.

Intention Creates & Destroys;
All intentions that are Good may seem to be Not-Good.

The Liberating Arts of Life & Death determine what is Good & Not-Good, by way of determining Net Good Outcomes.

If there is Good Intention, then there must be Not-Good Intention to balance it;
The North's Polarity is balanced by the South's Polarity;
With Positive Electromagnetic Fields, there are Negative Electromagnetic Fields;
The Universe is a Zero Sum of Intentional Balance;
If not, are there other Universes to Intentionally Balance this?

Cults of Personalities

Why worship Idols & Influencers & Individuals?
All worshipped from One, or worshipped One from All?

Worshipping One may be Not-Good;
Worshipping All may be Not-Good;
One worshipping One's Self may not be Not-Good.

Which One worshiped All?
Which One created Morals & Values & Beliefs?

Is One Recycling Morals that have been Recycled before?
Is there any new Moral to create?
Is every Moral already created?
Is every One borrowing every Moral?
Are All Morals passing through One as The Cycles Of Nature return?
Is Nature All?
Is Nature One?

Where do All Morals come from?
Where are All Morals going?

As water in a river passes, so too the Morals, Now.

Becoming

Beliefs: If, then; A way of The Philosophy.
Values: Reason, because; A way of The Artistry.
Morals: Good & Not-Good; A way of The Creatorship.

Beliefs for Good & Not-Good.
Values for Good & Not-Good.
Morals for Good & Not-Good.

One's Stage Of Life determines the Moral Outcomes.

Environment creates Thoughts;
Thoughts create Beliefs;
Beliefs create Values;
Values create Morals;
Morals create Creations.

An Athlete which never becomes a Philosopher values The Art of Body-Over-Mind;
Emotion over Thought.

An Athlete which never becomes an Artist values Mind-Over-Body;
Thought over Emotion.

Both halves are the same Brain, if working in Harmony;
If Brains are in Discord, Warfare is inevitable.

How quickly does Warfare separate the Brains!

∞

Training

The Coach is The Environment;
The Coaching is The Philosopher & Artist;
The Coached is The Athlete;
The Creation is The Trained Creator.

The Coached itself is an Environment;
The Coached is created by The Art of The Coach.

The Coach & Coaching are The Trivium & The Quadrivium;
The Persuading & Performing of a specific Practice, Hobby, Interest, Craft, and
The Similar, Ad Infinitum.

The Coach is The Creator of Environments;
The Creator of The Trained Creators.

Athletics is Good & Not-Good;
Philosophy is Good & Not-Good;
Artistry is Good & Not-Good;
Training is Good & Not-Good;
Creating is Good & Not-Good.

Choose Coach, conversely, Coached.

Worship

A book is a deity of grammar;
A library is a deity of knowledge;
A voice is a deity of melody;
A music instrument is a deity of harmony;
A bath is a deity of cleanliness;
A hospital is a deity of health.

Worship is everywhere One focuses;
Worship is everywhere One ritualizes;
Worship is everywhere One lives;
Worship is everywhere One dies.

To Worship is to Deify;
To Worship is to Create;
The One creates Deities;
The Deities are in One;
The One is the Deity Itself.

The Taxed & The Not-Taxed

Taxed, by way of Slavery;
Not-Taxed, by way of Servitude.

Religions can operate Not-Taxed;
Colleges can operate Not-Taxed;
Operating Systems can operate Not-Taxed;
Belief Systems can operate Not-Taxed;
Value Systems can operate Not-Taxed;
Moral Systems can operate Not-Taxed;
One Moral System can operate Not-Taxed;
All Moral Systems can operate Not-Taxed.

One can be Liberated from taxes, by way of serving One;
One can be Liberated from taxes, by way of serving All;
All can be Liberated from taxes, by way of serving One;
All can be Liberated from taxes, by way of serving All.

Govern-Ment is Controlling-Mind;
Slavery is being governed;
Servitude is self-governed.

Serve, by way of One's Moral Compass;
Slave, by way of Another's Moral Compass.

Slavery is Theft of Thought & Emotion & Creation;
Servitude is Gift of Thought & Emotion & Creation.

∞

Free Will

At what point is Free Will?
At Sensory Input?
At Sub-Consciousness?
At Consciousness?
At Conscience?
At Relative Perspectives?

Some say Environment determines Free Will.
Some say Thought determines Free Will.
Some say Emotion determines Free Will.
Some say Creation determines Free Will.

What is free to be Willed is Willed to be, freely;
What is freely Willed to be is Unknown;
What is Unknown can not be freely Willed;
What is not freely Willed is not Free Will.

Free Will & Will Power is relative to those Freely Willing, Now.

Liberty

One needs to be able to do what One wants to do;
One needs Growth & Governance of Good Morals;
One then Contributes to the Net Good Outcomes for All.

One needs to pursue Growth by Self-Governance, for all Growth is Self-Governance;
One needs to Grow & Govern One's Environment, Philosophy, Artistry, and Creatorship;
One needs to observe that this Growth & Governance is Infinite Life & Death;
All are Growing & Governing Morals;
The One is Infinitely Becoming One's Infinite Possible Morals.

One's Liberated Attention is One's Liberated Belief;
One's Liberated Belief is One's Liberated Focus;
One Liberated Focus is One's Liberated Value;
One's Liberated Value is One's Liberated Energy;
One's Liberated Energy is One's Liberated Life & Death;
One's Liberated Life & Death is All.

One's Environment is One's Body;
One's Body is One's Home;
One's Home is One's Liberation;
One's Liberation is One's Life & Death;
One's Life & Death is One's Liberty;
One's Liberty is One's Servitude;
One's Servitude is One's way of The Liberating Arts of Life & Death.

Infinitely Extraordinary Now

Belief in an Extraordinary Deity beyond the reach of Ordinary Human requires
Extraordinary Evidence.

Necessity gives birth to the creation of new ideas, inventions, and innovations.

Human is not born perfect;
Human needs to be guided;
Constantly redirected, until Unconscious Self-Discipline is Life Itself;
Life is Constant Change, so how can One be born Constantly Static, perfectly?

Reflections from the water are the past;
The mirror reveals the past;
The mind reveals the future;
The body creates the Now;
Now immediately becomes the past.

Creating is Living Now;
Now is Creating the Past;
The Future does not exist until Now is created.

∞

Resistance

All is Liquid;
Liquid is Water;
Water creates One;
One creates Ember:
Ember creates Fire;
Fire creates Wind;
Wind creates Resistance;
Resistance creates Ambition;
Ambition creates Passion;
Passion creates Persistence;
Persistence creates Creatorship;
Creatorship creates All.

Wind is Resistance;
Fire needs Wind to grow;
Rejection is the Wind for The Embers of One's Creation.

Balance

Flows & Ebbs;
Expansions & Contractions;
Peaks & Troughs;
How does One's pendulum change The Tide?

One's Fingerprints determine Imprints;
One's Imprints determine Expressions;
One's Expressions determine Expansions;
One's Expansions determine Contractions;
One's Contractions determine Dexterities;
One's Dexterities determine Agilities;
One's Agilities determine Strengths;
One's Strengths determine Fortitudes;
One's Fortitudes determine Characters;
One's Characters determine Creations;
One's Creations determine Outcomes;
One's Outcomes determine All;
All is Balanced Matter.

Balanced Matter determines Electrical Fields;
Electrical Fields determine Electromagnetics;
Electromagnetics determine Environments;
Environments determine Thoughts;
Thoughts determine Beliefs;
Beliefs determine Values;
Values determine Actions;
Actions determine Habits;
Habits determine Characters;
Characters determine Creations;
Creations determine Matter;
Matter determines Balance;
Balance is All.

Producing

Productivity is determined by Harmony of The Liberating Arts of Life & Death;
Harmony of Environment & Philosophy & Artistry & Creatorship.

Technological Advancement is determined by The Creatorship;
The Creatorship exists, by way of The Quadrivium;
The Quadrivium exists, by way of The Trivium;
The Trivium exists, by way of The Environment;
The Environment exists, by way of The Nature's Laws;
The Nature's Laws exists, by way of The All of Alls.

The Trivium is where Philosophers agree on Grammar & Logic & Rhetoric;
The Quadrivium is where Artists agree on Arithmetic & Geometry & Music &
Astronomy;
The Creatorship is where The All agree on One's Creation.

To be able to Understand & Overstand something, One need-know its Trivium;
To be able to Craft & Produce something, One need-know its Quadrivium;
To be able to Innovate & Invent something, One need-know its Creatorship.

High Quantity produces High Quality, by way of The Law Of Probability.

Producers Produce which leads to a Production of Products.

Reproducing

Be The Creator of Environments;
If One cannot be The Creator of Environments, be The Artist;
If One cannot Artistically create Environments, be The Philosopher;
If One cannot Philosophically create Environments, be The Environment;
If One cannot Be The Environment, there is The Absence of Free Will;
If One has no Free Will, The Law Of Probability creates One.

One Reproduces One's Morals;
A Compass exists without A Navigator;
Countless have Become of This.

How many will reproduce Truth?
How many will reproduce Good?
How many will reproduce Not-Good?

Erosion

The Vision is clear;
The Outcome is not-clear;
Light exists, then is non-existent;
What happens?

Air erodes All;
Water erodes all;
Heat erodes all;
Life erodes all;
Death erodes all;
How does One discover this?

As One begins, breathlessness baffles;
As One enters, embers engulf;
As One approaches, ambition ascends;
As One concludes, cognition consumes;
As One enlightens, expectation erodes.

Is This what One Envisioned?

Dissolving Universe

A chunk of salt in water;
A source of smoke into air.

Ocean Waves Crash & Flow;
Retracts & Dissolves into Earth.

Water Expands onto the seashore sands;
Water Retracts, then flows Onward;
Water Expands, then evaporates Upward;
Water Retracts into The Planet Downward.

Mist & Air seem to defeat gravity;
Time Dissolves Somewhere.

All will Dissolve Downward & Onward & Upward;
One Dissolves into All.

Will All Dissolve into The All?
Nothing escapes Dissolution & Gravity.

Becoming Infinity

One must Awake; One must Erect.
One must Push; One must Give.
One must Pay; One must Invest.
One must Time; One must Measure.

One must Lay; One must Sleep.
One must Pull; One must Receive.
One must Accumulate; One must Return.
One must Dissolve; One must Create.

Beginning to Die; Dying to Begin.
Eternal Awakening; Eternal Sleeping.
Time must Dissolve; Time must Sleep.

One & All must; All & One must.

The Truth will release The Unwilling's Will Free.

One & All

Concluding The Beginning of Now:
If One has tried to Understand & Overstand this text up until this point, then an
Infinite supply of questions may have become Created.

One must not believe all that has been felt;
One must not believe all that has been thought;
One must not believe all that has been expressed;
One must not believe all that has been created.

One Wills, if One must;
One must, if One Will;
One must Will, if One must be One, Now.

Deciding, Now:
After reading these Conceptualizations, One chooses to believe or not to believe the
Words of these Writings.

No Translation of these Writings can be claimed as The Original Grammar & Logic
& Rhetoric;
The Translation is the Translator's Moral decision of Grammar to translate.

If One decides to believe any Conceptualizations written here, then it becomes a part
of the Consumer's Moral Compass;
The Consumer can decide to Believe or Not-Believe;
Whatever One's Moral Compass is Now will have chosen a different future of Nows.

The Beliefs will Create Values;
The Values will Create Morals;
The Morals will Create One & All;
It will be Willed-To-Become One & All's Infinite Moral Compass.

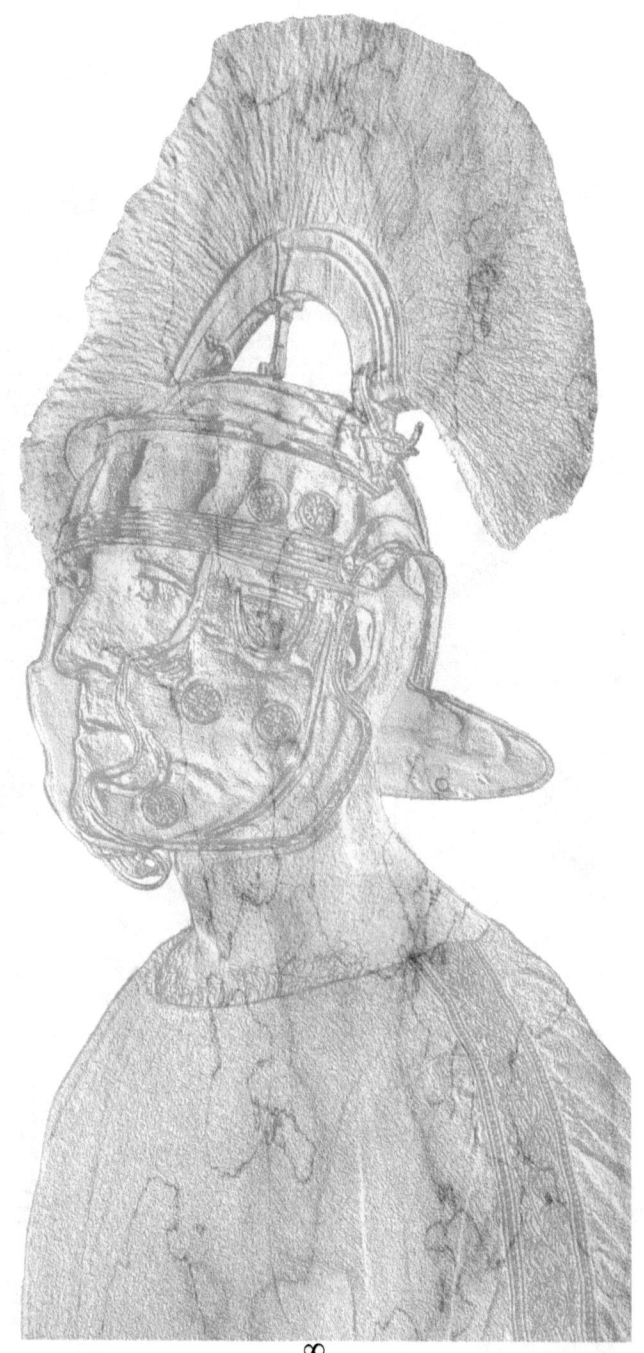

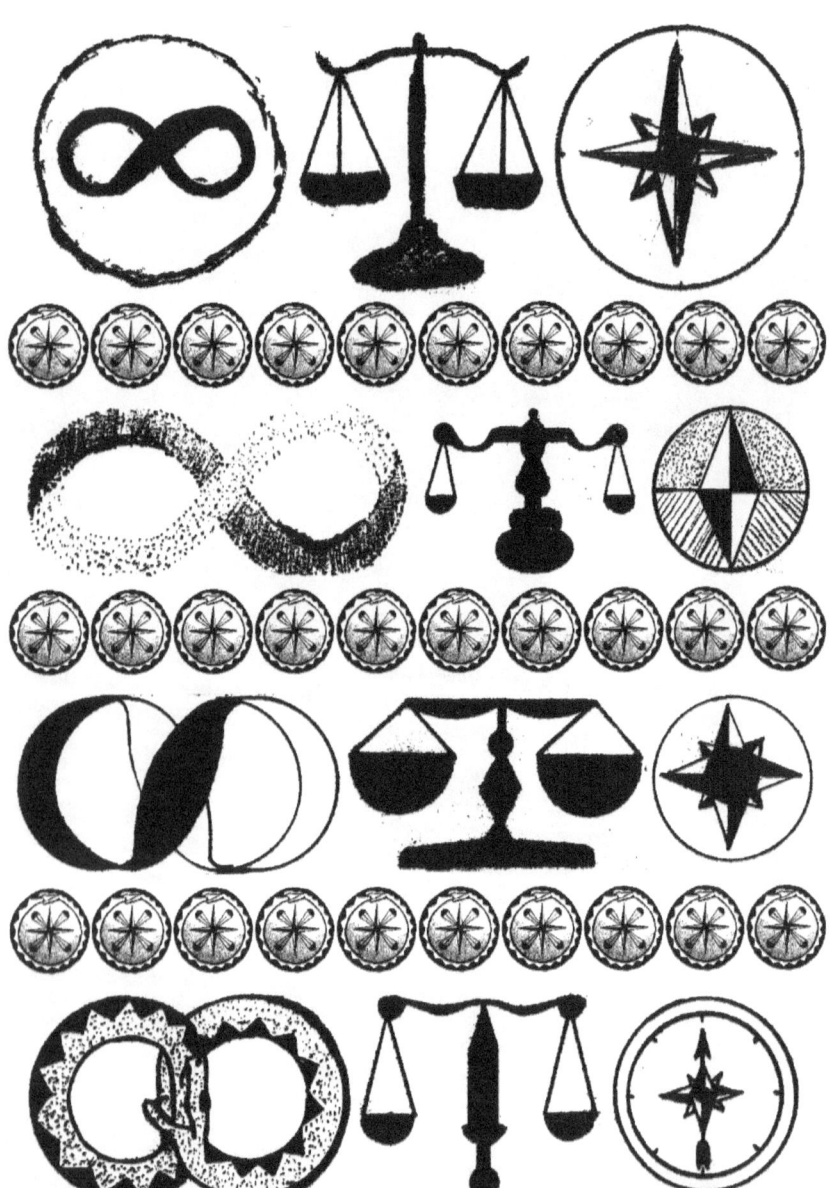

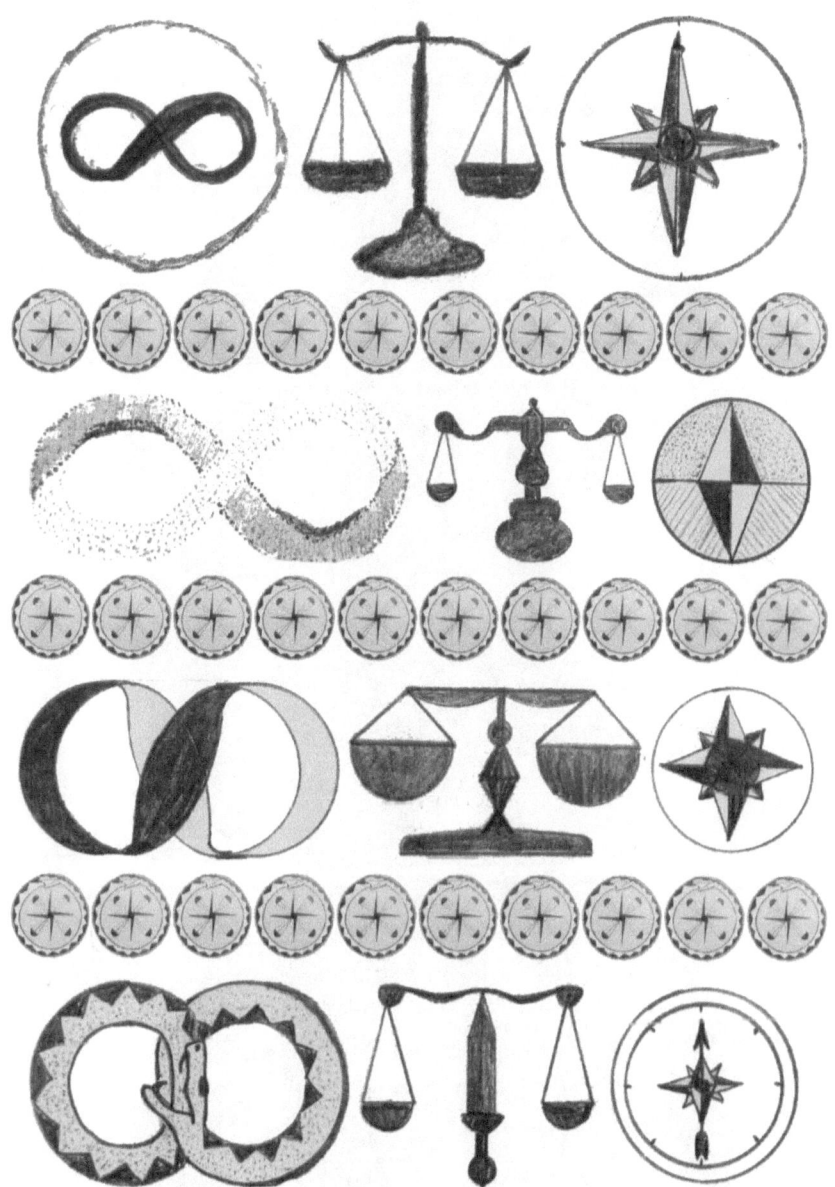

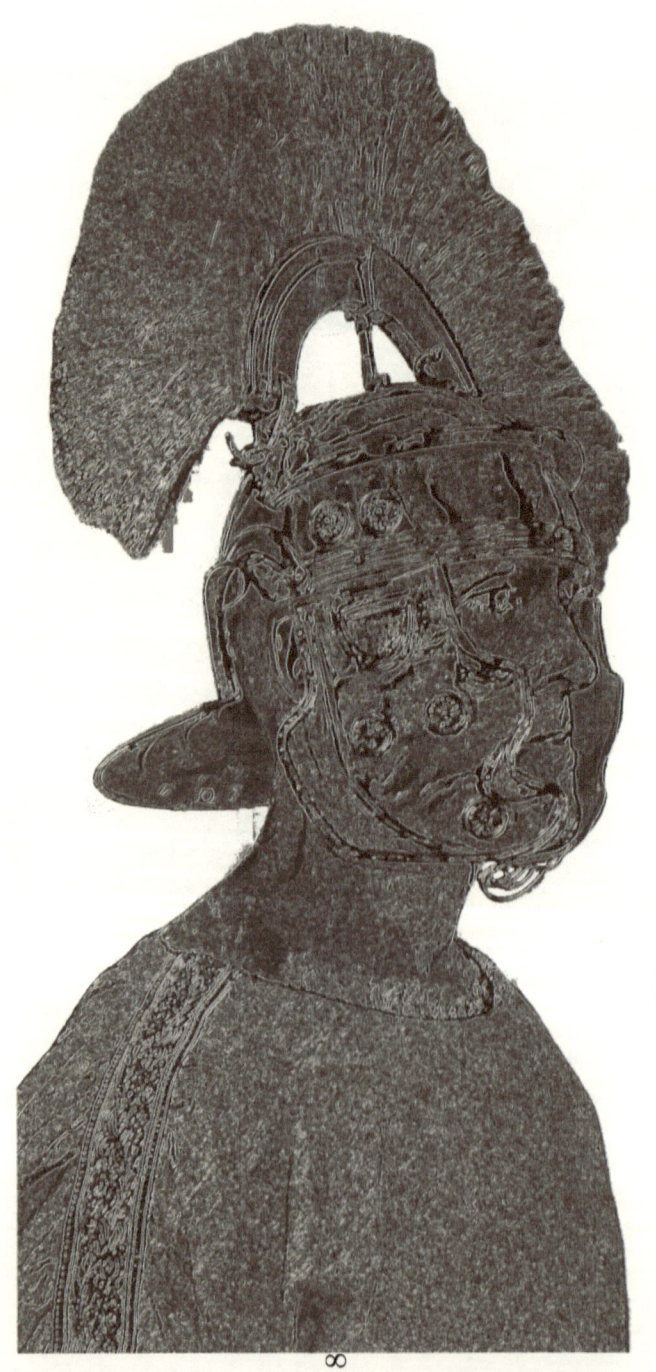

www.ingramcontent.com/pod-product-compliance
Lightning Source LLC
Chambersburg PA
CBHW030703220526
45463CB00005B/1875